MW00815593

Becoming a
CHAMPION
of CHANGE

How to Build
Support for
HR Initiatives
and New
Programs

M. MICHAEL MARKOWICH, D.P.A.

About WorldatWork°

WorldatWork is the world's leading not-for-profit professional association dedicated to knowledge leadership in compensation, benefits and total rewards. Founded in 1955, WorldatWork focuses on human resources disciplines associated with attracting, retaining and motivating employees. Besides serving as the membership association of the professions, the WorldatWork family of organizations provides education, certification (Certified Compensation Professional — CCP°, Certified Benefits Professional — CBP™ and Global Remuneration Professional — GRP°), publications, knowledge resources, surveys, conferences, research and networking. WorldatWork Society of Certified Professionals and Alliance for Work-Life Progress (AWLP) are part of the WorldatWork family.

Any laws, regulations or other legal requirements noted in this publication are, to the best of the publisher's knowledge, accurate and current as of this book's publishing date. WorldatWork is providing this information with the understanding that WorldatWork is not engaged, directly or by implication, in rendering legal, accounting or other related professional services. You are urged to consult with an attorney, accountant or other qualified professional concerning your own specific situation and any questions that you may have related to that.

This book is published by WorldatWork. The interpretations, conclusions and recommendations in this book are those of the author and do not necessarily represent those of WorldatWork.

© 2004 WorldatWork
ISBN 1-57963-1320

No portion of this publication may be reproduced in any form without express written permission from WorldatWork.

**The Professional Association for
Compensation, Benefits and Total Rewards**

WorldatWork
14040 N. Northsight Blvd., Scottsdale, AZ 85260
480/951-9191   Fax 480/483-8352
www.worldatwork.org

WorldatWork Staff
Publishing Manager: Dan Cafaro
Graphic Designer: Kris Sotelo
Production Manager: Rebecca Williams Ficker
Staff Contributors: Betty Laurie, Andrea Ozias

Technical Reviewers
John A. Kosky, CCP
Jane A. Montvilas, CCP
Andrew Moore

Table of Contents

Preface

Changes to HR programs often are viewed as controversial and difficult to implement. However, highly respected HR professionals have the reputation of knowing how to get things done that are critical to a company's success. Examples include:

- A compensation system that motivates employees to higher productivity

- Health and welfare designs that control costs, while providing employees with safety-net protection

- Disciplinary/grievance procedures that are perceived as fair by the workforce and give managers necessary tools to address "problem employees"

- Work-life programs to help employees balance work and non-work pressures, while assisting the company meet production needs

- A paid time off program to control costs of unscheduled absences, while giving employees flexibility to take time off to meet personal needs

- An orientation program that is perceived as having high value by workers and management

- Hiring approaches that enable the company to attract necessary talent in cost-effective ways

- An educational program to assist workers to better plan and manage their retirement.

A characteristic of top HR professionals is the ability to overcome resistance and find ways to win support from employees affected by new ideas and programs. "Customers," as used in this publication, refer to various constituencies the HR professional needs to service. Customers include everyone from the board chairman to entry-level workers, governmental regulators and other outside groups.

HR professionals should not only be the messengers, but leaders of change, especially changes that ask employees to act or behave differently. For example, change that:

- Requires employee participants to pay more for medical benefits
- Modifies behavior through wellness programs
- Increases salary based on pay for performance models instead of traditional base pay models.

Because many initiatives involve significant changes, success is not always guaranteed. Therefore, HR professionals are at risk. This publication highlights ways to increase odds to win support for your new ideas and programs to help your company. Strategies and tactics described are applicable to all industries, regardless of company size, location, profit status, or whether the workforce is unionized. Examples are based on actual experiences of HR professionals.

Think about this: Your company can have a great product or service, but if your company's customers do not purchase it, what is its value? Likewise, you, as the HR professional, can have a great idea to help your company, but your idea only becomes valuable if your proposal finds its way into your customers' hands and they end up liking it.

Introduction

Early in my career, my manager sent me to a two-day workshop on selling techniques. I questioned why I, as a director of personnel (before "HR" replaced the term "personnel"), needed to know how to sell. My boss said, "Go, anyway."

At the beginning of the course, the instructor asked participants to raise their hands as he mentioned various sales titles to gain a sense of the audience. At the end, he asked if anyone had a title that was not mentioned. I was the only person to respond. When I said, "director of personnel," everyone looked at me like "what is he doing here?" I really wondered what I would learn, and how I could use it.

When the workshop was over, I concluded it was the best course I had ever attended. Although none of the traditional HR topics was covered, it had everything to do with personnel or HR. The course focused on how to get to "yes." I learned that convincing customers to buy your product or service is an art. It's not easy, but there are ways and they work. After the seminar, I committed to learning more about effective ways to sell and obtain buy-in for new ideas.

When I refer to selling techniques, I am not talking about high pressure or calling people during dinner hours. Instead, I am referring to building momentum for ideas over time. Convincing your customers to accept new ideas results from facts, candor, building a relationship based on trust, and persuasive skills.

During my career I have taught graduate courses in management and HR at Temple University School of Business (Philadelphia). I primarily taught night school classes in which most of the students worked during the day. I quickly realized the students were struggling with how to achieve buy-ins and overcome resistance to change at their work sites. In response, I included practical "how-to's" in the curriculum because the textbooks were very light on how to implement changes.

Over time, I found high value in knowing how to use the selling techniques I had learned. The knowledge helped me to effect numerous changes as a director and vice president of HR at various companies. In 1990, I decided to start my own HR consulting company. As a consultant, I'm really a commissioned salesperson because I have no guaranteed income. As you can imagine, selling tactics and strategies have been most helpful.

Finally, I find many successful HR professionals feel comfortable with sales concepts as a roadmap to obtain buy-in for new ideas and programs.

The Golden Era

Some say this is HR's golden era. Companies need HR leadership more than ever. A key to success is to know how to overcome resistance and achieve buy-in from those affected.

As Machiavelli wrote in *The Prince*, "There is nothing more difficult to carry out, nor more doubtful of success, nor more dangerous to handle, then to initiate a new order of things." Or, as economist John Maynard Keynes stated, "The difficulty is not with new ideas, but in escaping old ones." These are reasons why people resist change.

The futurist and author Alvin Toffler provided some guidance. Toffler said, "Change is unlikely unless those who are affected perceive the new way of doing things as a workable alternative to the existing structure." This is the end result of buy-in.

The models, strategies and tactics presented are designed for the long run. In essence, this is not a 100-yard dash. It's more like a full marathon. Success is based on thinking differently, rather than how you probably were taught.

College HR textbooks are insufficient to help HR professionals understand how to successfully effect changes. In contrast, the one source of credible information I found helpful was in sales training literature. Yet, how many HR professionals see themselves as salespeople? Probably very few; however, you will find sales terms used in HR literature (e.g., influence, buy-in, persuasive skills, overcome resistance to change, new way of thinking, and relationship building). Perhaps knowing how to sell is not that radical for HR professionals.

1

Simple vs. Complex Sale

Simple Sales

The most common sale is the *simple sale*. In a simple sale, the buyer has complete power to buy. The salesperson's goal is to close the sale in almost any way. In essence, the end justifies the means. Success often is based on the salesperson's skill at one-to-one selling. In these situations, the salesperson has one chance to sell the product or service to a customer. Sales opportunities arise through telephone solicitations (often at dinner time), door-to-door selling, e-mail or shopping in department stores.

Simple sale approaches usually consist of high-pressure and manipulative techniques. Customers often end up annoyed and angry. If they buy, many experience "buyer remorse" and return the merchandise, or they make the purchase *despite* the approach of the salesperson. It is no wonder that selling has a bad connotation. Salespeople can end up having an image of a slick, fast-talking con artist — not the image HR professionals want to have.

Complex Sales

The more difficult sale and the one HR professionals are involved in is the complex sale. The sale results from a consultative approach based on earned respect and confidence in the seller. In a simple sale, customers often hear "Do I have a deal for you!" In contrast, the goal of a complex sale is for the customer to say, "Your product/service makes sense. Thanks for taking the time to help me decide the best option."

With complex sales, the objective is for the buyer to purchase the service. However, it makes no sense for the buyer to purchase the product and then return it due to buyer remorse. Therefore, with complex sales, the first step is to determine if the idea or initiative provides value to the customer. If not, then the HR professional should consider other options for the client. Success is based on mutual trust and respect that also are the hallmarks for HR success.

A client called me about developing literature to be mailed to employees' homes to announce a new benefits program. The HR professional wanted the material to convince employees of the new program's value. My response was for the company not to spend money on the mailing idea. I felt it would backfire. Employees might have become uncomfortable with the initiatives because the company wanted employees to take more responsibility for selection and payment of benefits. Also, employees might have questioned why the company spent so much money on the mailing, especially because employees would be paying more for benefits.

Instead, I suggested a program to assist employees in becoming smart benefits shoppers. Because the company wanted employees to be more active players, it was necessary to help workers understand their new role and how to continue receiving their safety-net benefits in a way that they could afford. The HR professional felt comfortable with this alternate approach that proved very successful and was less costly than the initial mailing idea.

Sometimes the best way to earn a customer's respect and be viewed as credible is to conclude the recommendation may not be in the customer's best interest and withdraw the proposal. This possibility would be an anathema in a simple sale. However, in a complex sale, the HR professional's goal is to build a long-term relationship based on integrity and partnership with customers. The objective is not to sell at any cost, but to have repeat business from clients based on a proven track record.

For example, the no-fault absentee control program is an alternative to address sick time abusers. A key component is consistency in the application of disciplinary action based on the plan's definition of excessive absenteeism. A possible client liked the no-fault concept, but felt strongly about having an internal committee of employees and managers to have the final say about any pending suspension or discharge. In essence, the committee would decide whether to implement the recommended action. This counters the key component of plan "consistency." Although the internal committee may make sense for the company, it places the company at risk of a charge of favoritism that could engender legal issues. Therefore, I withdrew the proposal because I did not want to support a plan that could become problematic for the client.

When the focus of a sale is customer-driven, selling does not have to be painful or uncomfortable. Instead, it can be rewarding and fun, especially as customers recognize the HR professional's value as an astute problem solver.

Another characteristic of the complex sale is the approval that is needed from many different customers. Any one influential person or group could veto the proposal or significantly delay the "buy" decision. HR professionals typically need buy-in at many levels, including:

- The board of directors
- Top management
- Middle management
- Affected employees, which can include part or the entire workforce
- Union officials, if organized.

One key person can either make or break the sale. To compound matters, the HR professional may not have direct access to all key decision-makers, such as board members. In this case, the HR professional needs a "champion" — often the HR professional's boss — to convince key decision-makers to support the proposal. Convincing many people or groups takes time, explaining why complex sales may take years before being finalized.

I once conducted a sales training seminar for a company that was in the relocation business and was having difficulty getting new business. It became clear that the salespeople at the seminar viewed HR professionals as the key decision-makers. Although HR professionals impact the decision-making process, the final say is usually made at higher levels within a company. The key to success was to have HR professionals serve as champions to promote the company with top management. This insight prompted the relocation company to adjust their sales strategies.

In this example, the relocation company's inability to earn new business was primarily due to thinking it was involved in a simple sale when, in fact, it was involved with a complex sale. The same mental roadblock can apply to HR professionals. I often hear HR professionals become frustrated when their recommendation dies on the boss' desk even if the boss likes the idea. What many HR professionals do not understand is getting the boss to say "yes" is often the first of many such steps.

HR professionals do not view their proposals as threats, but customers might. Any time an HR professional asks someone to accept a new program or idea — even if the initiative will be beneficial to employees — the affected employees are being asked to change. We might be in an era of change, but most people initially dislike doing things differently. People like staying in their comfort zone and see anything outside it as a "danger zone."

HR professionals may not consciously think of new ideas as having negative consequences. Nonetheless, a critical component of successful complex sales is to have people affected by the change accept the potential upset as a preferred trade-off to other options. Because people react differently to change, the possibility exists that someone will view recommendations as threatening, while the HR professional may see the proposal as extremely beneficial. For example, surveys highlight high percentages of employees who refuse "free money" from companies. These workers forfeit employer matches of individual contributions by not participating in a company's 401(k) program. Because these workers may have considerable influence over the eventual outcome of the initiative, the HR professional should be sensitive to negative feedback.

An inexperienced HR professional may underestimate the power that people or groups have to undermine a proposal, especially if benchmarking industry practices supports the new initiative. HR professionals often attend national conferences to hear speakers discuss implementation of programs that the HR professional's company wants to put in place. The HR professional is excited and returns with a handout explaining "what to do" and cannot wait to get to work. What happens? Frequently, the HR professional will hear how the company is different than the company used in the conference presentation. If this roadblock sounds familiar, then facts are not the cause, but rather the key decision-maker's interpretation of how the proposal affects his or her perception of how and what should be done.

2

Three-Phase
Internal Change Model

Professional sales managers invest considerable time and money to help their sales forces succeed with complex sales. Success at complex sales is difficult even for seasoned salespeople. It is no wonder HR professionals have problems obtaining support for initiatives and new programs. HR professionals are dealing with the most demanding type of sale, but most are not even aware of their dilemma. Compounding the problem is the expectation of success without being sufficiently prepared for the task of convincing others to support new ideas and programs.

The following will help fill the void:

Phase 1: Prospecting

"Find the itch, then provide the scratch," is an analogy that fits well when discussing the importance of prospecting, which involves locating needs and providing appropriate solutions. How the HR professional identifies "itches," or needs, is critical.

Historically, HR professionals were told what to do and when to do it. Today, top executives want HR professionals to be leaders of change, not just followers of directions. This means getting out of the office to interact with customers. This helps to build important relationships with different customers groups.

A colleague, for example, would have coffee with the maintenance staff at 6:30 a.m. in the employees' cafeteria. The half-hour of "small talk" before the start of the shift was my colleague's way of building relationships with this key group of customers. She knew the day would come when she had to talk "business" with the maintenance staff. She wanted them to know her as a person and not just the HR

Figure 1

**Phase 1
Prospecting**

**Find the Itch,
Provide the Scratch**

⬇

Get to Know the System
- Understand company culture, customs and rituals
- Obtain visas
- Build personal relationships

⬇

Identify Customers and Needs
- Who wants change?
- Who's concerned about change?
- Historic perspective
- Plant seeds

⬇

Understand the Power Structure
- Identify key decision-makers
- Identify influencers

professional. She believed in the value of the saying, "People buy from those they know and trust."

Salespeople know the value of "relationship selling," and it is just as important for HR professionals. The following are key steps:

Step 1: Get to Know the System

HR professionals need to understand the "why" behind company policies and practices, especially those labeled as "crazy" by the workforce. The HR professional's boss or current executive may have promoted the "crazy" policy. Senior employees in the HR department could be a good source for historical information. Knowing the policy's champion may keep the HR professional from stepping into a big pothole, and instead enable him or her to develop a more effective change strategy. At times, architects of policies become very defensive if someone tries to change what they think is brilliant.

To counter the possibility of defensiveness, HR professionals have found it helpful to first talk informally with the policy's architect. The discussion focuses on the need to modify the practice due to changes in the business environment. In this way, the HR professional is not directly attacking the policy but highlighting what has occurred to warrant modifying the practice, which also would be in the company's best interest. This type of lobbying is very effective for winning support, especially from those who backed prior practices.

Step 2: Identify Customers and Needs

During this step, HR professionals should interact with key customers to build relationships for future discussions. Key customers include:

- Top executives
- Middle managers
- "Swing people" (influential nonmanagement workers, sometimes referred to as "opinion leaders").

Building relationships begins with asking to meet customers in their own offices. People are more relaxed in their own settings. The visits also give HR professionals exposure and opportunities to tour different areas of the company. The initial goal is to learn how you can assist the customer. This is also known as prospecting.

Visiting customers is a quick way to learn what they need from HR, and to share some ideas and approaches on how HR can be of greater value to them. HR professionals who are established in their positions may want to use this approach to expand services in areas that they serve. With external sales, this outreach is known as expanding one's territory by adding new clients.

Having good relationships with swing people or opinion leaders is very important to the HR professional's success. These nonmanagement workers can influence or sway the opinions of others. You may not have many swing people, but every company has them. For example, if there are 100 employees in your company, you may have two or three swing people. If you have 1,000 employees, you may have nine to 12 swing people.

New HR professionals should schedule meetings during their first week of employment to meet and talk with the company's swing people. The meetings should be about 10 to 15 minutes in duration and held in your office since most swing people do not have their own offices. The purpose is to understand how these key customers view the HR program. This essentially is a data gathering session. The HR professional listens while the swing person talks. The HR professional also can convey approaches that have been effective at prior employers for reaction by the swing people.

One colleague (a new HR director) told me she found the swing people to have low confidence in her predecessor to fairly handle employee grievances. In response, she asked the swing people to "get the word out" that she was committed to having workers treated fairly. To convince workers, she asked swing people to encourage employees to talk with her about their grievances and then decide whether her actions were fair. She knew she had to establish employee confidence, and the quickest way was for swing people to get the word out. Within a week, employees began discussing grievances with her. The strategy worked, especially because she was able to win employees' confidence about her commitment to be fair.

Step 3: Understand the Power Structure

HR professionals need to understand how decisions are made. While the formal organization chart is instructive, there is likely an informal structure that has considerable impact. The formal chart shows who reports to whom, but it does not necessarily show who can influence decision-makers. Knowing those influencers can help the HR professional implement recommendations.

If you can earn the respect of influencers, those influencers could become messengers to help convince decision-makers. Professional salespeople have used influencers for years — they are called third-party referrals.

An early mentor told me that the three most important people for one's success are the parking lot attendant, the telephone operator and the boss' secretary. Technological changes have replaced the parking lot attendant and telephone operator. But having a good relationship with the boss' administrative assistant is still important, especially if he or she manages the boss' schedule.

Phase 2: Decision-Making Process

Step 1: The End Result of Successful Lobbying
A well-known sales axiom is: "Executives will support your proposal for *their* reasons more so than *yours*." The statement means that, while your proposal might be good for the company, it may be ignored unless decision-makers accept your reasons as valid. Therefore, before presenting a proposal, it's important for the HR professional to conduct a successful lobbying effort. By lobbying, I mean to actively involve all critical parties that can influence the final decision. Failure to include "key players" may result in a delay or even a rejection of a good idea. Remember the axiom, "people support what they help to create." Lobbying will take time. However, champions of change understand the value of time investment as a means to build support.

To assist the HR professional with lobbying activity, two worksheets are provided. (See Figures 3 and 4.) Figure 3 identifies four key decision-making players (ultimate decision-maker, influencers, technical advisers and customers) and Figure 4 helps you assess their feelings about a proposal. A brief description of each player follows:

Ultimate Decision-Maker
This could be the HR professional's boss, the boss' boss, the CEO, the board or a company committee. Determining who has final authority to release money to support the proposal or who has the final say to grant the request can identify the ultimate decision-maker.

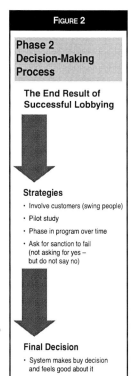

FIGURE 2

Phase 2
Decision-Making
Process

The End Result of
Successful Lobbying

Strategies
- Involve customers (swing people)
- Pilot study
- Phase in program over time
- Ask for sanction to fail
  (not asking for yes –
  but do not say no)

Final Decision
- System makes buy decision
  and feels good about it

Customers Affected by the Proposal

Customers could include: all workers, a certain group of workers, all managers, a certain group of managers, one company division, etc. Determining who will be affected by the HR initiative can identify customers.

Influencers

Influencers can be determined by identifying to whom the decision-maker listens before making a final decision. Also, determination can be based on who has direct access to the decision-maker.

Other influencers can be nonmanagers who are respected by their peers. Politicians label them as centers of voter influence. As mentioned in Phase 1, these swing people often are asked to join important company task forces because executives realize their support is important. At times, some swing people also can be technical advisers. When this happens, swing people have considerable say over what gets done.

Technical Advisers

These are employees upon whom the ultimate decision-maker may call for technical or professional advice. They could include:

- Internal auditor
- Payroll manager
- Chief financial officer
- Marketing director
- Legal counsel
- Computer support specialist
- Consultant
- HR professional
- Communications director.

Determining who will be asked to make judgments about the technicalities or legalities of an HR initiative can identify technical advisers.

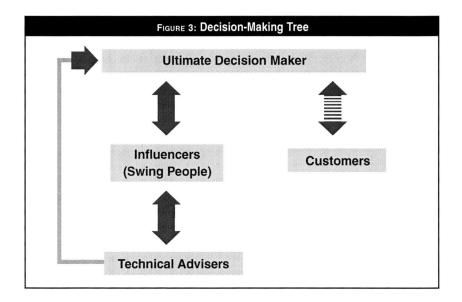

FIGURE 3: Decision-Making Tree

Ultimate Decision Maker

Influencers (Swing People)

Customers

Technical Advisers

Step 2: Strategies

Marketing executives understand the value of involving customers to test ideas before finalizing a new service or product. The same logic applies to HR initiatives. It is advisable to convene a task force of customers, especially *swing people*, to assist with the design and implementation of new programs. If the task force buys/supports the new program, then others should. If the task force identifies features that concern them, then it's better for the HR professional to be aware of the concerns as soon as possible so the issues can be addressed. It's like the Pennzoil commercial — "pay me now or pay me later."

When do you want to learn how employees feel about the new program or idea — before or after the proposal is final? Most people will say "before" to provide time to make modifications, if appropriate. At the minimum, knowing any negative feelings gives the HR professional an opportunity to speak to employee groups even if the final decision is to make no changes. People respect candor and become upset when management plays "dodge ball" and does not respond to specific questions or concerns.

Another common practice with complex sales is to *phase in aspects of the new program over time*. This provides time for the company and HR professional to assess the initiative's impact without risking everything at once. A further alternative is to use a *pilot study*. The HR professional could test a new idea or

	Strategic Assessment								
	S		**N**		**O**		**C**		
	a	b			a	b	l	m	h
FIGURE 4: Decision-Making Tree Worksheet									

	S		N		O		C		
	a	b			a	b	l	m	h
1. Ultimate decision-maker:									
Name: _____									
Title: _____									
2. Customers:									
Name/title: _____									
Name/title: _____									
Name/title: _____									
3. Technical advisers:									
Name/title: _____									
Name/title: _____									
Name/title: _____									
Name/title: _____									
4. Influencers:									
Name/title: _____									
Name/title: _____									
Name/title: _____									
Name/title: _____									

Place an asterisk next to any technical adviser who also is an influencer.

Key:

S = Supportive
    a = believes idea is good for the company
    b = feels the idea will be personally beneficial

N = Neutral = could be for or against the idea; decision is based on what other key players do

O = Opposed
    a = believes idea is not good for the company
    b = feels the idea will not be personally beneficial

C = Credibility (of the HR professional)
    l = low
    m = moderate
    h = high

Completing the Decision-Making Tree Worksheet

The HR professional should complete a decision-making tree. After writing in each person's name and title, the HR professional should determine whether the person is supportive, neutral or opposes the HR initiative. This is an initial assessment. Furthermore, it's important to identify the reason(s) for being supportive, neutral or opposed to the new program. Options provided are:

- The idea is good/bad for the company

- The idea is/is not personally beneficial to the person.

The final action is for the HR professional to assess the degree of credibility the HR professional has with each person (e.g., low, moderate or high). Credibility is important because it determines the HR professional's ability to influence that person. People who view the HR professional as highly credible will tend to accept recommendations much more quickly than those who do not.

The HR professional probably will have varying degrees of credibility with different people. Therefore, it is important to identify people who influence the key players who view the HR professional with lower credibility. Finding and winning over those who influence key players are critical components to managing complex sales successfully.

People who are neutral can be swayed based on how other key players feel about a recommendation or may be influenced by new information. The HR professional needs to develop a strategy to identify what is needed to gain a neutral person's support, just as it is important to figure out how to address or minimize opposition.

The assessment of key players' feelings is fluid. Changes need to be made as additional information is obtained. It is important to focus on uncovering key players and to determine their feelings about any proposal, especially how they feel the HR initiative will affect them. Politicians realize voters support the candidates they feel will best represent their interests. HR professionals need to realize their customers will support proposals if customers believe new programs or ideas are in their best interests.

approach with a smaller group or perhaps with one division of a multi-site company. The HR professional most likely would work with a group receptive to the change. It's akin to first opening a show off-Broadway. Changes can be made based on customer feedback before deciding to open on Broadway. In essence, customers really are supporting what they helped to finalize. Customers now have some ownership of the final product.

Sometimes the best strategy is *not* to ask for approval, but to ask for *sanction to fail*. This is a "hard-ball" strategy and should be used only when you have exhausted all other strategies. It's high risk, but can give you the "green light" to proceed. The downside is you may be risking your job.

But isn't this what many top executives often do? The risk can be great. But reward for accomplishment also can be great.

Step 3: Final Decision

If the decision-making process is handled well, obtaining the green light to successfully implement new initiatives should be a logical conclusion. The decision-making process highlights the initiative's value to customers and the company. Because key players are actively involved in the design and implementation, most customers will end up looking forward to the new program. In essence, key players are supporting what they helped to create.

Phase 3: Postmortem

Buyer Satisfaction, Not Buyer Remorse

Just because a program is successfully implemented does not mean the project is over. Sales professionals know the importance of an initiative living up to its expectation. Also, programs that meet expectations are a salesperson's best referral for more business.

For HR professionals, successful initiatives are the best way to establish and enhance credibility. The next time the HR professional submits a recommendation, decision-makers will be more receptive to support it. Past successes will earn the HR professional additional power and respect.

FIGURE 5

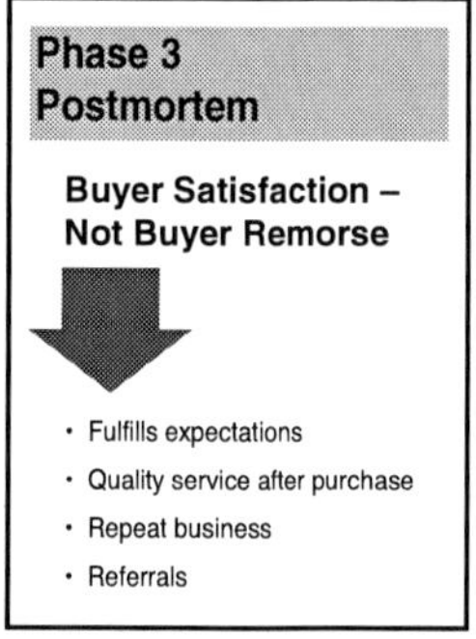

Phase 3 Postmortem

Buyer Satisfaction – Not Buyer Remorse

- Fulfills expectations
- Quality service after purchase
- Repeat business
- Referrals

Follow up with periodic reports highlighting the initiative's impact. There is nothing better than quantitative reports — those featuring hard numbers, especially financial data or employee attitude percentages — to show the value of any change. Qualitative reports, which consist of feedback from surveys and focus groups, also should be encouraged. The combination of qualitative (soft data) and quantitative (hard data) reports gives HR professionals an excellent "one-two" punch.

3

8 Practical Tactics to Enhance Key Relationships

1. Eat lunch with different people in the employees cafeteria.

A 30-minute lunch each day equals 125 hours of annual networking. Sales professionals understand the value of "breaking bread" with potential customers. Likewise, the HR professional can build good relationships with many people during lunchtime.

2. Have early-morning coffee at the "watering hole."

People tend to be more relaxed when having coffee before work. This is another opportunity to build relationships.

3. Participate in company social and athletic events.

Employees tend to see others as "real people" at company social and athletic events. We all play a role while at work — it's called our job description. But, once we're outside our role, we often are perceived as more human. Also, these activities tend to equalize employees. Instead of "the boss," you become just another player on the team. Many executives like opportunities to interact with workers in fun activities.

4. Send "thank you" notes.

An HR professional received a "thank you" note from an employee whom she had thanked for serving on a company task force. The employee was touched by the HR professional's thoughtfulness. The worker said he had served on numerous company task forces during his 15 years of employment with the company. The HR professional's thank you note was the first time management ever thanked him for his time and effort.

5. Make plant rounds.

These visits are an effective way to make contacts. Respond quickly to comments or questions regarding HR practices to establish and enhance your image as a responsive executive.

6. Challenge your staff.

A new HR director changed the negative feelings employees had about the HR department's response time. The new director told employees of her commitment to quick and accurate responses to questions about HR policies and practices. She asked employees to call the HR department with any questions and, if they were not satisfied with the response, to call her.

In the interim, the new director told her staff of this commitment. She also conducted in-services with her staff so they could respond quickly and accurately to employee inquiries. The new director's gambit worked. Her staff appreciated having the chance to show how good they were.

7. Prepare the soil before planting seeds.

Floating a "test balloon" can be a useful way to identify a new project or idea without formally asking for approval or even an opinion. HR professionals can mention a new idea or approach learned at a conference or from a professional journal article to a key customer. The purpose is to "float" the idea without trying to push it. Reactions will help the HR professional gauge initial feelings and decide next steps.

Many HR professionals make the mistake of submitting a proposal too quickly. It is important to assess the company's readiness and willingness to change before proceeding with the selling process. Also, the HR professional needs to line up allies to support changes. Submitting a proposal is relatively easy — submitting one that gets approved takes a lot of work.

8. Be sensitive to customers with veto power.

An HR professional related how a CEO's executive assistant delayed implementation of a revised company-wide compensation program. All levels signed off on the proposal. However, the HR professional made a fatal mistake. The CEO's executive assistant was classified at the second highest administrative support level instead of being at the top — or in a separate category. The HR professional learned too late that the executive assistant had "veto" power.

4

The Power of Asking
the Right Question
at the Right Time

omplex sales questions are designed to move people through various phases in the decision-making process. Making the decision to move ahead with a plan comes naturally when you ask the right question at the right time. It is as if the decision to support HR initiatives just evolves — it makes good business sense.

The questioning process provides important tools for HR professionals to navigate through decision-making steps. Winning support for new ideas and programs is not a matter of luck or good timing (although luck and good timing never hurt). It is the result of a carefully planned strategic approach. Timing is important, but should be considered as only one aspect of the strategic plan.

With complex sales, it is necessary to clearly understand key players' perceptions and ultimately provide them acceptable ways to meet their needs. This can occur by asking the right question at the right time. One case is Ronald Reagan's question during the 1980 presidential campaign: "Are you better off today than you were four years ago?" The question made people think and some campaign experts submit that this one question clarified why voters should vote for Reagan — which they did. Questions have power. The key is to know what to say and when to say it.

If asked correctly, questions can enhance the probability of sales success without alienating other people. Even if the eventual response is "no," an HR professional does not want to burn bridges because a "no" today may become a "yes" tomorrow. A colleague told the story of how he lost a contract to another consulting company. His usual manner was to thank the possible client for the opportunity to submit a proposal and, if circumstances changed in the future, to contact him. Most times, he never heard from those potential clients. However, he sometimes received a call asking if he was still interested in the work. Occasionally, consultants who initially win the contract do not work out. Coming in second sometimes works. The key is to never burn bridges.

The following Five Question Cycle identifies a sequence of questions that will lead to obtaining buy-in for new ideas and programs. (See Figure 6.)

Phase 1: Ice Breaker Questions

These low-key questions are used to begin a discussion. The HR professional should be careful not to ask too many "ice breaker" questions because they can anger or bore the person being questioned. Examples include:

- How long have you worked for the company?
- Where did you work before coming to the company?
- How many employees work for the company?

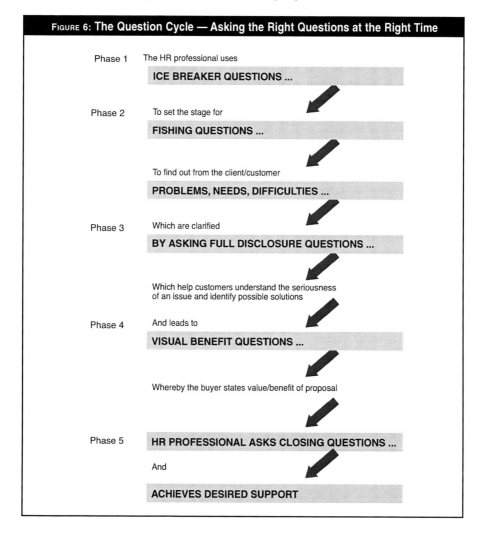

FIGURE 6: The Question Cycle — Asking the Right Questions at the Right Time

Phase 1 The HR professional uses
ICE BREAKER QUESTIONS ...

Phase 2 To set the stage for
FISHING QUESTIONS ...

To find out from the client/customer
PROBLEMS, NEEDS, DIFFICULTIES ...

Phase 3 Which are clarified
BY ASKING FULL DISCLOSURE QUESTIONS ...

Which help customers understand the seriousness of an issue and identify possible solutions

Phase 4 And leads to
VISUAL BENEFIT QUESTIONS ...

Whereby the buyer states value/benefit of proposal

Phase 5 **HR PROFESSIONAL ASKS CLOSING QUESTIONS ...**

And

ACHIEVES DESIRED SUPPORT

Phase 2: Fishing Questions

Fishing questions are asked to uncover potential problems, difficulties and dissatisfactions in areas where the HR professional can help. Answers give guidance to perceived needs and possible solutions. Examples include:

- What is the current absentee control program? How effective do you feel it is?

- What is the current pay system? Why does the company want to move to a pay-for-performance program? Who's promoting the change?

- Has the company ever tried to implement a pay-for-performance program? If yes, what happened?

- What's causing the low participation by nonhighly paid employees in the company's 401(k) plan?

- Have you considered wellness initiatives to help control your health costs? If yes, have you implemented any and what were the results? If no, what has prevented the company from moving ahead?

- What can my department do to better serve you and your workers?

HR professionals are encouraged to move quickly to fishing questions because they focus on the customer's issues.

Phase 3: Full Disclosure Questions

These questions take the customer's initial problem and explore the full effects and consequences of possible remedies. Full disclosure questions give customers a clearer understanding of the seriousness of the problem and identify possible solutions. Some examples include:

- What is the effect of reducing unscheduled absences by 10 percent or $500,000 a year?

- If employees understood investment strategies, would they increase their 401(k) contributions?

- Would management be willing to involve employees to design a program that would give workers extra money if bottom-line objectives were met?

Phase 4: Visual Benefit Questions

The stage is set for HR professionals to win tangible support for an action plan by addressing the customer's acknowledged need. It is particularly important for the customer to verbalize the benefits of adopting the new program. The HR professional wants customers to feel the new idea has value. The best way to know is for the customer to actually say so. Examples of visual benefit questions include:

- How does the new program appear to meet your needs?

- If a task force of employees feels positive about the financial education program, would you be willing to have it presented on company time?

- If the CFO believed the absentee control program would save the company money, could we review the proposal with a group of employees to work out the details?

- If we could structure a pay-for-performance approach that would not be an "entitlement" program, would we receive top management buy-in?

- Would you be willing to work with top management to develop a team incentive program in which employees would receive extra money for meeting documented bottom-line objectives?

Answers to these questions should lead the HR professional and customers to the final stage — the close.

Phase 5: The Close

A salesperson's ultimate goal is to close. However, in complex sales, the decision to accept the HR professional's recommendation seems to evolve naturally — it just makes sense to the customer. It is not a hard sell, but one the customer believes will address a pressing problem.

5

How To Communicate
Bad News

No one enjoys being the deliverer of bad news. But someone has to do it. It's not unusual for people to become angry when hearing bad news; therefore, it's important to address negative feelings at the beginning of the change process to diffuse any anger. To be successful as the "messenger," the following guidelines are recommended:

- Keep your message short. The goal is to convey facts with minimal embellishment.

- Explain "why" the company decided to make the change. The company's decision often is the "best in a series of bad options." For example, a company facing a large deficit may be forced to cut benefits or freeze wages. No one wants to hear this. However, if the alternative is to lay off workers, then cutting benefits or wages may be a viable option.

- Ensure that employees clearly understand how the change will impact them.

- Have face-to-face meetings with workers. Do not just rely on written communication.

In the 1990s, a *Fortune* 500 company announced it was terminating an important benefits plan and replacing it with an alternative. The company used e-mail and an internal Web site to announce the change. No employee meetings were held. The communication highlighted the benefits to employees of the alternative plan including a sizeable savings for the company. Unfortunately, the company did not make it easy for employees to understand the impact from converting to the new plan.

Company employees took it upon themselves to figure out the impact. Many workers became outraged when they discovered they would lose considerable coverage when compared to what they expected to receive under the original plan. In response, employees began communicating among themselves via a Web site to plan next steps. Due to the "employee revolt," the company eventually decided to modify its position.

Fallout from the company's decision to change the benefit arrangement caused:

- Intervention from governmental regulators to determine the appropriateness of the change.

- A serious union drive among company employees.

- Severe morale problems. Many workers felt personally hurt by what they perceived as the company's insensitivity to them and lack of candor by not explaining how the change would adversely affect them.

- The company to not save the money they had expected.

My own assessment is the company viewed the change process as simply telling employees what will happen — an example of "command and control" management. Unfortunately, the company actually was involved in a complex sale process but acted like it was a simple sale.

Early in my career, a mentor told me the more controversial the change, the greater the need to have face-to-face communication with employees before the change. Changes sometimes are initially perceived as takeaways or negatives. But direct interaction between HR professionals and workers should help employees understand the "why" for the change, positive and negative effects of the change, and how employees and the company can benefit from the change.

This type of interaction takes time. However, the end result is greater employee acceptance. Perhaps some good can come from the negative experience, especially if we can learn from the example company's mistakes.

6

Case Studies

T he following case studies are based on actual situations. They illustrate how HR professionals can effect changes by using the complex sales process. Some changes saved companies millions of dollars, while others ended up costing more money. However, companies viewed all the HR initiatives as necessary and important. Also, changes were controversial and took time to take effect. The end results were worth the efforts and enhanced the HR professionals' image as leaders of change.

Brief descriptions of HR initiatives are presented because the cases' main focus is to highlight how HR professionals won support for new ideas and programs. More information about design options used in the cases can be obtained by researching the WorldatWork body of knowledge.

Case Study 1: No-Fault Absentee Control Program

Phase 1: Prospecting

A new HR director of a manufacturing company of 750 employees started her employment by asking managers and swing people for their views of the HR program. Not having ownership of the past, it was safe to ask how others felt about HR's value to them. By using "fishing questions," the HR director found a need for a more effective attendance policy.

Managers complained that although the current practice rewarded employees with excellent attendance, it was ineffective against abusers. Employees complained the current system was administered inconsistently by managers and penalized employees with good attendance. It seemed abusers were able to take time off with pay whenever they wanted and good attendees ended up covering for the abusers. Top executives were concerned about the increased costs of employee absences and supported the call to do something. This historical perspective enabled the HR director to better understand what managers and employees were looking for and why.

The new HR director had found success with an approach she had implemented at another company: a no-fault absentee control program to manage and reduce excessive absenteeism. Although many companies and surveys report no-fault to be effective and supported by workers and managers, the concept is not without controversy and takes time to implement.

Phase 2: Decision-Making Process

The HR director decided to begin the change process by reporting her findings from talking with managers and employees at the company's HR committee (an advisory group of managers from a cross-section of the company). She highlighted the need for an improved attendance policy and explained concerns raised by staff about the current practice. She also presented the no-fault concept as a solution.

Presenting a solution may seem risky because the full committee had not heard the report prior to the meeting. However before the committee meeting, the HR director had talked with key committee members about her findings and recommendation of a no-fault approach. These members supported the no-fault suggestion and urged her to discuss the concept at the full committee meeting. With the additional backing of key members, the HR director felt confident to present the approach.

Although all members supported doing something, not all managers felt comfortable with the proposed solution. Some felt no-fault was "too off the wall" for managers and employees to accept. Others liked it. The HR director was not surprised by the mixed reactions. She had seen it before and knew what to do. This was a complex sale. Members needed time to think about the concept, which the HR director encouraged them to do. The committee would continue discussion at the next month's meeting. In the interim, the HR director asked committee members to talk with their supervisors and employees about the need for an improved attendance control policy and the pros and cons of no-fault.

The HR director left the meeting encouraged. The discussion was the first step to getting the program eventually implemented. Because no-fault was somewhat controversial, the HR director had expected some resistance. However, key issues were on the table and, most important, a "seed had been planted."

Some may question the merits of talking openly with workers about a controversial policy. I have found the grapevine will buzz about no-fault even if management tries to keep things quiet. Talking openly allows candid discussions about the need and reasons why no-fault could be the solution. Discussions held only on the grapevine tend to distort facts and give rise to greater resistance based on half-truths.

Between meetings, the HR director continued her lobbying efforts. She further reviewed the no-fault approach with line executives and other pivotal managers (e.g., payroll and data processing managers) whose support was necessary. The HR director knew it was important to personally find out who favored no-fault and who had reservations. Knowing how pivotal managers felt helped her better understand what she needed to do to eventually "sell" the program. This included those who also influenced key decision-makers.

At the next committee meeting, although the HR director sensed increased support, members still had mixed feelings. During her lobbying, the HR director found a group of managers and employees who wanted no-fault. So, she proposed a pilot test with a group of managers and employees who liked the concept. In this way, those who had reservations could wait for the outcomes, and those who favored no-fault could try it out. The committee supported the pilot, which also was endorsed by top management.

The next step was to convene a task force of managers and swing people to work with the HR director to finalize the policy. The task force took four months to develop the policy, and the pilot lasted one year.

Phase 3: Postmortem

At the end of one year, the task force and full committee reviewed the results of the no-fault pilot and made the decision to implement the program throughout the company.

In this example, the HR director was the facilitator of change. She was not seen as "selling" no-fault; although in retrospect, the best salespeople are rarely seen as selling. The need for change came from meetings with managers and employees. The HR director actively involved all key staff in the change process and she took the necessary time for the company to feel good about the change. Consequently, the HR director was seen as a problem solver and an agent of positive change. Isn't this what HR professionals are expected to be?

Case Study 2: An Alternative Rewards Program

Phase 1: Prospecting

Literature highlights the value of alternative rewards programs such as gainsharing, profit sharing, stock options and bonuses. The hope is employees will be motivated to find ways to enhance operations, especially if they can share in the "spoils." Alternative rewards programs are not without risks to company and workers. Particular concern is to obtain employee buy-in to the concept that additional compensation is not an entitlement, but rather is based on bottom-line results. This means employees must be willing to invest extra time and effort with no guarantee of extra compensation — not an easy sale!

The nursing executive of a community hospital of 800 employees talked with the HR director about establishing career ladders (a concept for nurses to advance over time with additional compensation at each step). The nursing executive was searching for ways to motivate her staff to greater productivity. She felt extra pay to compensate for additional responsibilities associated with a career ladder program would motivate staff to greater productivity.

The HR director had a different thought. Because patients are really taken care of by teams of caregivers, why not develop a program to reward team efforts, rather than individual efforts, for the enhancement of patient care? The reward for achievement of excellence would be extra money. The nursing executive liked the teambuilding idea, but questioned from where the money would come.

The HR director responded by outlining the following ground rules:

- **Rule 1:** Patient care improvements had to be supported by objective documentation.

- **Rule 2:** This was to be a team effort because the team takes care of patients moreso than any one person.

- **Rule 3:** Team members, along with the HR director and nursing executive, would develop patient care goals and ways to evaluate the attainment of objectives.

- **Rule 4:** Team members would be involved in the actual evaluation to determine if objectives were met.

- **Rule 5:** Reward money had to come from documented savings. The chief financial officer had to sign off before any extra money was distributed.

The nursing executive felt comfortable with the rules. Together they decided to test the ideas with her staff.

Phase 2: Decision-Making Process

Before meeting with the nursing staff, the HR director had to convince the hospital's CEO to support the concept. The CEO, who came from the school of "command and control," had mixed feelings. He did not want to pay staff extra money at a time when the hospital had fiscal problems. He also questioned why staff would be involved with a decision he considered to be management's. After reviewing the rules, the CEO, though still uncomfortable, allowed the process to continue because of rule No. 5. The HR director had used the tactic — "ask for sanction to fail (not asking for yes — but do not say no)." By having confidence in the change process, the HR director was willing to take the risk to avoid a "red" light from the CEO. The strategy worked. The CEO did not say "no."

The next step was to present the team reward concept to the nursing leadership. The group supported the idea and liked the five rules, especially the possibility to receive extra money. The HR director and nursing executive then presented the team reward concept to a group of nursing "swing" people. As expected, the group had many questions. However, the executives were selling *an idea — not a developed program*. Also, (this is a radical point) the employees were given the right to refuse to participate in the program. In essence, the nursing staff had the *veto power*! They could say, "we are not interested," and the idea would die on the table without any hard feelings.

The HR director and nursing executive believed that success was based on employee willingness to work with them. Together, they could develop something new. Stating the ground rules up front and giving workers right of first refusal go a long way to fostering the development of gainsharing programs.

Phase 3: Postmortem

As it turned out, the specialty care units (emergency unit, cardiac care, intensive care and operating room) decided not to participate. However, the medical/surgical units agreed to participate. It took about one year to develop the program. This was not a "hard sell" because the staff was not pressured into working with management. In contrast, managers and staff enjoyed working together to create something new and actually had fun developing the components of the team rewards program. Consequently, the program was successfully launched.

Success with alternative rewards programs is significantly influenced by employees' willingness to play by new rules. Clearly, there are many steps to building a successful alternative rewards program. Two crucial conditions are:

1. Employee acceptance that the program is not an entitlement

2. Employee and management's willingness to work together to develop the program's components, especially objective evaluation criteria that is supported by all involved.

Case Study 3: Paid Time Off (PTO) Program

Phase 1: Prospecting

The CFO of a municipality of 700 employees projects it will default on its bond issue within five years. The reason: The municipality cannot afford the payout of unused sick time for employees who plan to retire within five years.

The municipality has many long-term employees because it is seen as a good place to work. However, within five years, a high percentage of workers will be eligible for retirement. The CFO projects the cost from paying out unused sick time as cost prohibitive. The municipality cannot afford the costs without taking drastic austerity measures, such as layoffs, or raising taxes — two very unpopular options.

The municipality allows employees to carry over unused sick time to a maximum 1,400 hours. Employees are paid the unused sick time upon retirement. Payment is at the last hourly rate. The municipality viewed the program as an incentive for employees not to abuse sick time. Payout was not expected to be too expensive because benefits were viewed as a "fringe" cost. However, over time, "fringe" benefits became very costly.

Top management decided that something had to be done to avoid the projected fiscal problem. Raising taxes or laying off workers were not acceptable options. The HR director recommended ending the practice to pay for unused sick time upon retirement and implement a paid time off (PTO) bank (vacation, sick, and personal time lumped together into one bank of time). A benefit of PTO programs for employees is the ability to schedule time off regardless of reason.

Phase 2: Decision-Making Process

The HR director's first task was to convince top executives that PTO banks made sense. With the CFO's assistance, the HR director was able to convince top management of PTO's fiscal soundness. Some executives questioned the fairness to terminate sick time payout benefit upon retirement.

Many executives had vested interests to continue the practice. However, all agreed the municipality could not afford to continue the current practice, but differed on what changes to make.

The HR director suggested meeting with a group of swing people to explain the problem and present PTO banks and the capping of the sick time payout practice as the municipality's solutions. Based on feedback, the HR director would report to executives with any further suggestions. The HR director cautioned executives to expect employee resistance and to be prepared to seriously revisit some modifications to the proposed solution.

At the meeting of swing people, employees expressed anger about losing what many saw as a "promised" benefit. Employees spoke about being loyal to the municipality and now sensed top management was betraying them. Some employees openly stated interest to talk with a union to represent them because workers felt they could not trust management (the municipality was nonunion).

The HR director was not totally surprised with employees' reaction. Who wants to lose any benefit, especially a payout benefit upon retirement? Employees viewed sick time as theirs — either they used it while working or received payment upon retirement.

Effecting change often elicits negative feelings. Affected groups will fight to keep what they believe is due them. This is why few significant changes occur in the absence of economic pain. Just look at the problem the United States is having with financing Social Security. Any solution will engender resistance from those who will lose something. Eventually a remedy will be implemented. But it takes courage and skill to navigate through the "rapids." HR professionals are faced with similar challenges — not in the scope of Social Security — but surely to navigate through storms resulting from employee anger over benefits changes.

The key, as Alvin Toffler stated, is to provide a working alternative, and to help employees understand why change is in their best interest. This is the "Rubicon" for HR professionals. Those that have the savvy to manage employee resistance will earn the status associated with being a top executive. It's not easy, but can be done.

The HR professional again reiterated the problem the municipality faced and provided numbers and hard data to support the explanation. The HR director asked the swing people to think about what was discussed and to reconvene in two weeks to further talk about the problem and proposed solutions.

Between meetings, the HR director and CFO explored alternatives to the termination of unused sick time payout benefit. The CFO recalculated projected cash flow estimates for the next five years. The CFO concluded the municipality had sufficient reserves to pay out current balances if employees' unused sick time accounts were frozen until actual retirement. Employees would be paid for the balance of unused sick time based on hourly rates as of the effective date of capping the accumulation of unused sick time benefit. Payment would be made when employees retired. Top executives approved the modification based on the CFO's projection and interest to maintain good employee relations.

At the next meeting of swing people, the HR director presented the modified payout plan. Employees initially did not like having the payout based on their hourly rate when the payout plan would be capped, especially for employees who expected to work another five to 10 years for the municipality. However, employees expressed concern for the municipality's welfare. Being loyal, long-term workers, they wanted the municipality to remain a viable employer. What bothered the swing people was losing a benefit they felt they had earned. The modified plan preserved the benefit's value as of a specific date. Employees would not lose everything, as they initially feared. Consequently, swing people bought in to the modification and supported the PTO plan.

Phase 3: Postmortem

This is not collective bargaining. The municipality was not negotiating with a union. However, this author has found value in a "give and take" with employee groups, especially when employee acceptance for significant change is beneficial to the company. Particular emphasis is to identify key change features — referred to as "must have." In this example, eventual termination of payout benefit is a "must have." In contrast, flexibility is encouraged in other features referred to as "like to have" (e.g., timing of termination of payout).

Eventual supporters of change are long-term workers, although these employees might initially resist changes. However, their views can be turned around if they understand why change is necessary for the company's welfare.

This is where candor and facts can be most useful, in contrast to presenting a fancy slide show or mailing literature to employees' homes. Nothing can replace honest face-to-face communication, especially when employee support for difficult decisions is important. The HR director in this case was a true champion of change.

Case Study 4: Cafeteria "Flex Benefits" Program

Phase 1: Prospecting

A service company of 4,000 workers was faced with finding ways to lower costs by $5 million. The company prided itself in being an employer of choice and committed to employee job security. Consequently, the company had never laid off any workers. However, due to shortfall in revenue, layoffs seemed inevitable.

The HR director recommended implementation of a cafeteria "flex benefits" program as one option to save money. The company offered a rich benefits package and many workers had dual health coverage because working spouses also received health benefits from their employers. The HR professional saw an opportunity to lower costs by "incenting" workers to choose wisely from a menu of benefits, while paying workers extra money if they left the company's plan and were only covered by their spouses' health plan. The savings from leaving the company's plan would more than compensate for additional payout costs.

The company's benefits philosophy had been to provide the richest benefits package possible with minimum employee cost. The expectation was employees would want to work for the company. Consequently, the company had many long-term workers and low turnover. The benefits philosophy had worked. Unfortunately, introduction of new competition for customers and pressure to hold down prices of services caused the company to project losses of about $5 million. Times had changed. The company had to respond.

Phase 2: Decision-Making Process

The first step was to submit a proposal to the human resources committee of the company's board of directors. The HR director was able to convince the board members of the fiscal viability of "going flex." The HR director had worked closely with the company's CFO to develop the fiscal analysis. As expected, the CFO supported the report. Dealing with potential employee upset was another matter. Board members were concerned about adverse employee relations resulting from benefits changes.

The company had been very generous in paying about 95 percent of the health premiums. With the flex plan in place, employees would be expected to pay about $100 more a month for health and welfare benefits if they maintained their current high option plans. Moving to less expensive benefits options would enable employees to break even. However, employees would receive extra money if they opted out of the company's health benefits and went on their spouses' health plans.

The HR director's straightforward response to the board's concern was that it was his job to manage employees' reaction. In essence, the HR director was willing to put his job on the line to obtain board approval to move ahead with flex. The board gave the green light to move forward.

The next step was to convene a task force that became known as the Flex Team. The team's goal was to finalize all components of the flexible benefits program. One of the HR director's selling points to the board was the company was not going to use outside consultants to develop the flex program. This avoided a significant cost. The HR director felt confident that internal company staff had the skills necessary to make flex work. He also concluded that if company people were the architects, then it would be easier to implement flex. In essence, *people support what they help to create.* This became a key component of the HR director's selling strategy. Other members of the Flex Team included the directors of payroll, communications, management information systems, finance, internal audit, members of HR department, and a cross-section of line managers from key operations departments.

Because the Flex Team was comprised of managers, the HR director needed to involve nonmanagement employees. He convened another group of swing people (influential nonmanagement workers). Some executives were worried the swing people would be too difficult to handle. These executives advised the HR director not to convene the group. In contrast, the executives said to just let the Flex Team develop and implement the program. The HR director felt the advice seemed to reflect the "command and control" mentality that he philosophically opposed.

The HR director knew employee support was essential for flex to be successful. Managing expected employee upset meant interacting directly with workers in the same way companies test market new products with actual customers before formally launching new products. A strategy to manage expected employee anger was needed.

Before the meeting with the swing people, the HR director met with members of the Flex Team to conduct a "mock" meeting. Flex Team members were asked to list all questions and concerns they would have if they were swing people. The HR director wanted everyone to be candid. His strategy was to identify all "hot issues" and then develop a candid response for each one. The HR director wanted to be prepared for meeting with swing people.

At the beginning of the meeting, the swing people listened politely to the presentation. When the HR director asked for their reaction, they let him have it. It was as if the workers had not really listened to the "why" behind the change. Employees were angry and felt the company was not sensitive to their needs. Why, they asked, should employees pay up to $100 more per month for health and welfare benefits? Employees also were uncomfortable with having to choose between options. They did not like the change.

At this pivotal point, the HR director asked the task force members a full disclosure question, "What would they do if their rent went up 47 percent?" The question caused silence in the room. The HR director repeated the question. Employees answered by saying they would not accept it. They would try to get it reduced or they would look for another place to live. All employees agreed that a 47-percent increase was unfair. The HR director now had the opening he needed. He informed the group that the company's primary health care carrier had raised the premium by 47 percent. And the insurance carrier would not discuss reducing it. In essence, the insurance carrier told the company to "take it or leave it."

The explanation shocked the employees. A strange thing happened. The timing of the full disclosure question caused employees to replace their anger to the company with an open mind to further discuss the issues. Now employees began to hear the "why" behind going flex. Another meeting was scheduled to continue the discussion. By the end of the second meeting, the swing people accepted the change to flex as the best alternative, given the circumstances. In essence, going flex was the best in a series of bad options. With the swing people's support, the Flex Team finalized company-wide communication strategy. Members of the Flex Team and swing people assisted with the implementation — the flex program became theirs, not just HR's to be sold to workers.

The HR director believed it's easier for people to accept change if they first understand the reasons for the change and then, as Toffler advised, accept the new arrangement as an acceptable alternative. Sometimes it takes a well-timed full disclosure question to open minds to listen, especially if those affected are angry because of the change.

Phase 3: Postmortem

Implementation of a cafeteria "flex benefits" program is a monumental task, especially if the goal is to save money. You can expect employees to initially resist the change. The key is to build allies throughout the company and candidly confront hard issues with fact-to-face communication. Working with task forces of managers and swing people proved to be very effective.

As the media has shown, sampling of key groups can give a good indication of how the larger population may feel. The same applies with HR professionals attempting to implement changes. In this example, how the company went about implementing the flex program was essential to reaching acceptance by a diverse group of workers and ultimately, for its success. This was not an easy sale. But it was a complex sale that was effectively managed.

The HR director was willing to put his job on the line for the chance to prove he could do it. He had faith in the flex design and the ability of people within the company to work well together to make the project a success. He was comfortable with the complex sales process. As things turned out, he was seen as someone whose vision helped the company address a major problem. Employees appreciated keeping their jobs and found the flex program also met their safety-net needs.

Case Study 5: New Employee Orientation Program

Phase 1: Prospecting

A retail department store chain of 14 stores wanted to revamp its new employee orientation program. Feedback from past attendees reflected low value from attending. Managers did not want to send workers to the program because many employees complained it was a "waste of time."

Phase 2: Decision-Making Process

The HR director began her lobbying by talking with department store managers. She wanted to learn their specific concerns about the current orientation format and any ideas they had for improvement. Most store managers felt new employees did not need a company-wide orientation. The majority of managers felt each store could sufficiently orient new employees.

The chain's CEO supported decentralization, but felt there could be value to have a consistent corporate-wide message for new employees. He challenged the HR director to come up with something unique that the store managers also would support.

The HR director viewed the CEO's support and challenge as an opportunity. She decided to be daring and bold. Most traditional orientation programs (which she referred to as glorified newsletters) review benefits, safety and company policies. Instead, she decided to develop a seminar-like program that highlighted how employees can help the company remain profitable. This included:

- Explaining changes in the industry
- Impact of new competition
- How workers can respond if they hear people in their neighborhood complain about the company's products or services
- Company's commitment to handle work-related problems in a fair manner
- Why workers should buy the products they sell.

To test the market, she discussed her ideas with a few store managers. Managers were intrigued with her views and enthusiasm, but were not completely sold on the return from paying new workers to attend the half-day company-wide orientation.

In talking with the CEO about the store managers' reactions, she proposed a pilot to test the new format. Specifically, she requested approval to have three company-wide orientations, each held the first of the month for new workers who were hired the prior month. The workers would be asked to complete an evaluation at the end of each session. The results would be forwarded to the CEO and store managers. She asked the CEO to give a brief presentation at each orientation. The CEO agreed and suggested the HR director present the pilot idea at the next month's meeting of the CEO and store managers.

Before the meeting, the HR director explained the pilot idea with the store managers who she spoke with previously. They supported her idea and mentioned they would speak favorably for adoption by other store managers. The pilot idea was endorsed at the meeting. Having the CEO speak at the sessions also solidified his support for the pilot program.

Phase 3: Postmortem

Feedback from new employees was positive. Employees expressed appreciation of being told what the company was up against to remain competitive and how they could assist the company. Most said the orientation program was unlike any they had ever attended and helped them better understand the company's strategies for success. They also liked the complimentary lunch.

Case Study 6: Conversion from Advancement of Paid Time Off to Accrual System

Phase 1: Prospecting

A bank of 500 workers wanted to convert its paid leave benefits from being advanced every January 1st to an accrual system. The bank, like other companies, granted a full year's allowance of sick, vacation and personal time at the beginning of the calendar year. Some companies grant such time on each employee's anniversary date. If the employee left the company with a negative balance (i.e., employee had not worked long enough in the calendar year to repay paid time used), then the employee would owe the company the balance. In many situations, companies never collected the money.

To avoid losing money, the company decided to grant paid time off benefits on an accrual system. This meant an employee would receive 1/26th of vacation, sick and personal time every pay period (i.e., company paid employees on a bi-weekly basis).

Phase 2: Decision-Making Process

The HR director convened a taskforce of swing people to talk about the company's interest to convert to an accrual system for paid leave benefits. Many workers were familiar with the accrual approach because they had worked at companies that had such a method. However, the employees' major concern was they were used to receiving the advancement of time off benefits. Many employees, therefore, had planned vacations based on the advancement. How then would they be paid for scheduled time off if the company implemented the accrual system?

The HR director reviewed the employees' concern with the payroll director. Together, they came up with a strategy. Conversion to the accrual system would become effective January 1 — employees would receive four months of advance notice of the change. New employees hired on or after January 1 would earn paid time off on the accrual system. These employees would earn time, but would be eligible to use only earned time upon satisfactory completion of the company's six-month probationary period. Employees hired before January 1 would receive the advancement of paid time off granted January 1. However, the advancement arrangement would end effective the following January 1. Therefore, employees had one year to adjust their scheduling.

The HR director reviewed the proposed conversion idea with the CEO and CFO. They supported the idea. The CFO's support was influenced by the payroll director's involvement in coming up with the recommendation.

The HR director now interacted with the swing people. Concern was raised about allowing only one year to modify scheduling habits. It seemed many workers took time off in January for their annual vacation. Therefore, the group requested additional consideration. The HR director further investigated how many employees wanted time off in January. The number was smaller than originally thought. As a result, the HR director modified the time line to be 14 months instead of one year. The additional two months would accommodate workers who scheduled time off in January and February with extra flexibility. The company received what it wanted — support from the swing people to support the conversion plan.

Phase 3: Postmortem

Once the conversion process was complete, employees accepted the accrual system for paid leave benefits. The main reason: Converting to an accrual system reinforces what is normative at work — "you work and then get paid." So it makes sense to work and then accrue paid time off benefits.

7

Conclusion

Knowing how to sell is essential for HR professionals to win support for new ideas and programs. HR professionals who feel comfortable with selling see both visibility and being the messenger as important steps to build credibility. And credibility gives HR professionals the power to influence others to achieve desired goals.

The complex sales process is composed of a series of phases. It is rare that an initial discussion results in the acceptance of a new idea. Closing a complex sale often takes longer than expected and unforeseen obstacles are the norm. Therefore, a key ingredient for success is to know what questions to ask and when to ask them. It also is important to be patient because complex sales take time. It is not unusual for HR professionals to invest two to three years or even longer to convince all people necessary to implement a new program. This is why having the stamina of a long distance runner is important.

Numerous authors have stated that success in the Internet/Information Age requires a different way of thinking and behaving. A key strategic question for businesses is how to use human resources programs as motivators to achieve business objectives. Solutions will require challenges to habits and long-standing beliefs on how work should be accomplished and the obligations employers and employees have to each other. Therefore, a strategy to manage resistance to achieve desired objectives is needed.

So how can HR professionals win support for new ideas and programs in this type of climate?

The techniques, tactics and case studies described in this book will give HR professionals a jumpstart to learn necessary persuasive skills required for success. We know success in today's ever-changing business environment requires risk taking and new ways of thinking. The radical thought for HR professionals is to view sales acumen as an essential skill for success as a leader of business change.

Appendix

HR professionals who want to learn more about complex sales and the art of persuasion should consider the following suggestions:

- If your company has a sales force, ask to attend a sales in-service training session and read articles about selling in sales journals.

- Consider attending a seminar on how to sell, sponsored by external sales trainers.

- Read books on selling. (See "Suggested Reading" list.)

After doing your research and homework, try out what you've learned. It may seem awkward at first, but don't give up. Keep on trying. You'll eventually succeed. Remember, most people fall off a bike at least a few times before mastering it. However, once you learn how to ride a bike, you never forget how to do it. Just as riding a bike is fun, so too can you enjoy the success from knowing how to persuade others to accept your new ideas and programs. Good luck!

Suggested Reading

SPIN Selling by Neil Rackham

The Sales Bible: The Ultimate Resource by Jeffrey Gitomer

Guerrilla Selling by Bill Gallagher

The Power of Persuasion by G. Ray Funkhouser

How to Master the Art of Selling by Tom Hopkins

Strategic Selling by Robert Miller and Stephen E. Heiman

How to Work a Room: The Ultimate Guide to Savvy Socializing in Person and Online by Susan RoAne

You Can Negotiate Anything by Herb Cohen

The Perfect Sales Presentation by Robert Shook